GALAXY OF SUPERSTARS

Leonardo DiCaprio

Hanson

LeAnn Rimes

Spice Girls

Jonathan Taylor Thomas

Venus Williams

CHELSEA HOUSE PUBLISHERS

GALAXY OF SUPERSTARS

Jonathan Taylor Thomas

John F. Grabowski

CHELSEA HOUSE PUBLISHERS
Philadelphia

Produced by
21st Century Publishing and Communications
a division of Tiger & Dragon International, Corp.
New York, New York
http://www.21cpc.com

Editor: Elaine Andrews
Picture Researcher: Hong Xiao
Electronic Composition and Production: Bill Kannar
Design and Art Direction: Irving S. Berman

CHELSEA HOUSE PUBLISHERS

Editor in Chief: Stephen Reginald
Managing Editor: James D. Gallagher
Production Manager: Pamela Loos
Art Director: Sara Davis
Director of Photography: Judy L. Hasday
Senior Production Editor: Lisa Chippendale
Publishing Coordinator: James McAvoy
Cover Illustration: Brian Wible

Front Cover Photo: Kimberly Butler/London Features International, Ltd.
Back Cover Photo: Photofest

The Chelsea House World Wide Web site address is
http://www.chelseahouse.com

First Printing

1 3 5 7 9 8 6 4 2

Library of Congress Cataloging-in-Publication Data

Grabowski, John F.
    Jonathan Taylor Thomas / John F. Grabowski.
    p. cm.—(Galaxy of superstars)
    Includes bibliographical references and index.
    Summary: Biography of the teen actor whose starring role on
television's "Home Improvement" and voice of Simba on the big
screen's "The Lion King" have made him known as "JTT" to fans.
    ISBN 0-7910-5150-1 (hc)
    1. Thomas, Jonathan Taylor—Juvenile literature. 2. Actors—
United States—Biography—Juvenile literature. [1. Thomas,
Jonathan Taylor Thomas. 2. Actors and actresses.] I. Title. II. Series.
PN2287.T365G73 1998
792'.028'092—dc21
    [b]   98-44424
                                                                        CIP
                                                                         AC

CONTENTS

1

THE PEOPLE'S CHOICE

The year 1997 was exceptionally rewarding for Jonathan Taylor Thomas. His hit television comedy, *Home Improvement*, was in its seventh successful season for the ABC network. The show was continuing its remarkable run as one of the most popular shows on TV. And *Home Improvement* had recently been honored in a special Showcase event by the Academy of Television Arts and Sciences.

The cast and production team continued to receive recognition for their excellent work. Several members received nominations in various categories for both Emmy and Golden Globe Awards.

The show's success had catapulted Jonathan to stardom and to status as a teen heartthrob. It also helped him on the road to a career in the movies. His latest film, *Wild America*, had been released just that June.

With his popularity on the rise, Jonathan was in great demand. He felt it was his duty to give as much of his time as possible to the many charities with which he was involved. The young actor always tried to do as much as he could to help those who were less fortunate than he. In

As Randy in the hit television show Home Improvement, *young Jonathan Taylor Thomas captured the hearts of viewers, particularly his teen fans, who chose him as their special heartthrob.*

October, Jonathan appeared with *Home Improvement* costar Taran Noah Smith on *Nickelodeon's Big Help-A-Thon,* an event sponsored by Nickelodeon (the TV network especially for youngsters) and the YMCA to encourage young people everywhere to volunteer time to their communities.

As if that were not enough to keep him busy, he was also offered many opportunities to do guest shots on various TV shows. In 1997 alone, he appeared on *The Tonight Show with Jay Leno, Nick in the Afternoon, CBS This Morning, Entertainment Tonight, Fox After Breakfast, Access Hollywood, Late Night with Conan O'Brien, Live with Regis & Kathie Lee, The Late Show with David Letterman,* and *The Rosie O'Donnell Show,* among others.

One other such opportunity came Jonathan's way in early April 1998. He was offered a spot as a presenter on *Nickelodeon's 11th Annual Kids' Choice Awards* program. Nickelodeon held a yearly show on which it presented awards honoring the favorite shows and celebrities of that year. Awards included those for Favorite Movie, Favorite Movie Actor, Favorite Movie Actress, Favorite Television Show, Favorite Television Actor, and Favorite Television Actress. The field of music was not left out of the proceedings either. There would be awards for Favorite Musical Group, Favorite Song, and Favorite Singer. Other trophies would include a wide range of subjects such as Favorite Sports Team, Favorite Cartoon, Favorite Animal Star, Favorite Book, and Favorite Video Game. Talk show personality Rosie O'Donnell was to host for the second consecutive year.

Jonathan arrived at UCLA's 12,000-seat Pauley Pavilion, where the show was to be held. This was not a brand new experience for him. About a year and a half earlier, he had been a presenter at the 1996 Emmy Awards and also at the Family Film Awards that same year. This time, he was scheduled to give the award for Favorite Movie Actress.

In 1996, Jonathan was a Kids' Choice nominee in the category of Favorite Television Actor,

Sometimes referred to as the "Home Imps," Jonathan (right) and his Home Improvement brothers, Zachery Ty Bryan (center) and Taran Noah Smith (left), share the spotlight at a Kids' Choice Awards ceremony.

Jonathan has not let his popularity go to his head. He is gracious with others and at ease in the public eye, even when surrounded by the media, as he is here being interviewed.

but he did not win. He was nominated once again in 1998 for his role of Randy Taylor in *Home Improvement*. The other nominees were Tim Allen, also of *Home Improvement*; Kenan Thompson and Kel Mitchell of *Kenan & Kel*; and Marlon and Shawn Wayans of *The Wayans Brothers*. *Home Improvement* was also nominated for Favorite Television Show, and Tim

Allen for Favorite Movie Actor for his role in *Jungle 2 Jungle*.

When it was time for the presentation for Favorite Television Actor, Jonathan held his breath. He didn't really expect to win the award—not with such tough competition.

Then came the big moment. The winner was . . .

"Jonathan Taylor Thomas!"

Jonathan was quite surprised and thrilled to hear his name called. "This is awesome," he said, "a huge honor."

In accepting the award, he thanked all the special people in his life, particularly his mother and the rest of his family and friends. He dedicated the award to his grandmother, who was celebrating her 94th birthday that very day.

The award had a special meaning since it was voted on by five million fans who took part in the nationwide poll. Jonathan was officially one of the most popular young male entertainers in show business and, arguably, the top box-office attraction among young teenage audiences.

2

FROM PENNSYLVANIA TO CALIFORNIA

Bethlehem, Pennsylvania, is a quiet town of 70,000 located in the eastern portion of the state. The town is in one of the largest steel-producing regions in the United States, and many of it's residents work for the giant Bethlehem Steel Corporation.

In 1981, one of the company's employees was Stephen Weiss, whose family had settled in the area many years before. Stephen was an industrial sales manager with the company; his wife, Claudine, was a social worker. Their first child was a three-and-a-half-year-old boy named Joel Thomas. Then, on September 8, 1981, the family increased in size when Claudine gave birth to a second son. They named the boy Jonathan Taylor.

Jonathan likes to say that he's "like Heinz 57 . . . a mix of everything." Part of his ancestry is Portuguese. "That's where I get the olive skin," he says.

People always tell mothers how beautiful their babies are, but in Jonathan's case, they did not lie. He was a beautiful, blue-eyed, blond-haired baby whose smile simply lit up a room.

Jonathan's road to success began when his family relocated from their Pennsylvania hometown to California. He enjoys a special relationship with his mother, Claudine, who taught him to think of others first and who has encouraged and supported him in his career.

Jonathan was a naturally friendly child, both with adults and with other children. At a very young age, he gave indications of having above-average intelligence. He was an early talker, and he carefully observed everything that went on around him.

His parents, as well as others, were amazed at his maturity, noticing that he acted like someone much older. His mother once remarked, "At eighteen months old, Jonathan seemed older than his age, and he was really outgoing. Everyone kept saying, 'Wow! Why don't you put him on television?'" Little did she realize how prophetic those words would be.

From an early age, Jonathan was taught that people were the most important thing in a person's life. Through Claudine's work, Jonathan came into contact with many physically and mentally challenged individuals. The youngster noticed how his mother gave so much of her time to others, and it had a lasting effect on him. He has never forgotten the lessons he learned when he was young. Jonathan was taught that no matter how unfortunate a person may be, that person is still deserving and worthy of respect. As he says today, "My mom just brought me up to care about others." This appreciation and caring for others is what drives Jonathan today to donate so much of his time to charities.

Like many other children his age, Jonathan had dreams of his own. Perhaps because he heard others say it so often, one of his ambitions was to be on TV. Thousands upon thousands of children have a similar goal. For most of them, however, it is nothing more than a dream. As they grow older, other things become more important, and the dream is eventually forgotten.

But not with Jonathan, who, even as a child, showed a determination that was unusual in someone so young. An example of this was his decision to become a vegetarian. At the age of four, he found himself eating less and less meat. His mother is a vegetarian, and perhaps part of his decision was based on what he saw. Says Jonathan, "When I sat down and realized what I was eating, what I was putting into my body, realized it wasn't good for me. That's the thing. I didn't feel well when I ate this stuff—I got headaches from it. So I said, 'What am I getting out of this? A little flavor that lasts for a second?' So I just dropped it."

Jonathan stood firmly by his decision. Today, as a teenager, he especially enjoys Greek and Italian food and eats mostly salads, pasta, tofu, and vegetables. Red meat never passes his lips.

It was around this time that Jonathan's family arrived at a decision which would affect his life in many ways. They moved to a suburb of Sacramento, California, a much larger city than Bethlehem, with a population of nearly 375,000. It is one of the fastest-growing cities in the country and an ideal place to raise a family. Located near the intersection of the American and Sacramento Rivers, Sacramento lies between the Sierra Nevada mountain range and the Pacific Ocean. Because of its position, many recreational activities are available within a short distance. Skiing, boating, camping, rafting, and fishing are just a few of the more popular ones. Nearly 400 miles from Los Angeles, Sacramento is still closer to that center of the television and movie industries than the east coast town of Bethlehem, Pennsylvania.

Long before he became a teen idol, Jonathan's infectious smile and outgoing, generous personality brought him many friends in school and on the athletic field.

Sunny California was a big change from sometimes-dreary Bethlehem. Stephen had a new job as an industrial sales manager, and Claudine continued her social work. The two boys found themselves in new surroundings and among new faces. For Jonathan, the new surroundings offered new opportunities—such as the chance for him to pursue his dream.

Jonathan's new hometown had an excellent school system and many organized sports for the boys to become involved in. Both Jonathan and Joel were very athletic and quickly became active in competitive athletics on the soccer field. Jonathan joined a neighborhood team when he was just five years old. He picked up the finer points of the game almost immediately and soon became one of the better players on the squad.

His involvement in sports provided Jonathan with an added benefit. As a member of a team, a player has to learn to take directions from the person in charge—the coach. This requires discipline, an important ingredient necessary for success in any field.

The effect of learning discipline would soon be seen in the classroom. Jonathan began school at six, and right away showed an aptitude for reading, writing, and math. Jonathan not only showed a strong interest in learning but seemed to be curious about everything. When he was placed in the advanced group, he was doing work far above his grade level.

The concern for others which Jonathan learned at home made him popular with the other kids and with his teachers. One day, he was given an assignment which required him to make a list of six of his friends. When it was time to present it to the class, he was worried that the kids he did not mention would feel left out. He began by explaining to everyone that he was still friends with them all, even though he had to limit his list to six.

Around this time, Jonathan developed a keen interest in a hobby which has remained a favorite of his to the present day—fishing. Jonathan spent several weekends fishing on lakes in the Sacramento region with his brother and father. The boy learned to love these peaceful breaks from his regular routine of school and his sports.

When Jonathan takes an interest in something, he tries to learn as much as he possibly can about the subject. Fishing was no exception. While most kids his age were reading comic books and picture books, Jonathan began getting fishing magazines, which he still collects. "I've been reading fishing magazines since I was five," he reports.

Reading fishing magazines had an added benefit. In addition to teaching Jonathan more about his hobby, it also helped him develop his reading skills. This, in turn, has helped him with his school work.

Young Jonathan's life was becoming very full. School work, soccer, and fishing were all making demands on his time. Little did he know, however, that this would be nothing compared to his life in a few short years. A great change would come about because of something he happened to see on television.

3

DEDICATION AND HARD WORK

O ne day, when he was six years old, Jonathan happened to see something on the TV screen that caught his eye. A commercial was advertising a course which could show a person how to get into commercials. Jonathan still remembered his dream of some day appearing on TV, and he somehow sensed that this might be a way for him to attain that goal.

Jonathan's mother, naturally, was skeptical at first. When he continued to badger her, however, she gave the idea some thought. After some research, she decided that the company doing the advertising was reputable, and she enrolled Jonathan in the 13-week course.

The course helped the youngster develop his natural talents and abilities. He learned how to pose for the camera and how to model clothes. He learned how to project his confidence to viewers and how to develop a "stage presence," or awareness of an audience.

After the course was completed, there was a graduation ceremony at which each of the students showed what he or she had accomplished. This was especially important because local talent scouts were in the audience. One

Incredibly mature for a boy his age, Jonathan was poised and confident when he began modeling kids' clothing. Through his determination and hard work as a young model, he would soon fulfill his early dream of appearing on TV.

scout from San Francisco's Grimme Agency was so impressed with Jonathan that he offered the boy a modeling contract. Although San Francisco was not quite the same thing as Hollywood, it was a good starting point. Despite some reservations, Jonathan's mom let him sign up with the agency. His career in front of the camera was underway.

Modeling was not easy work, and it sometimes required many hours of traveling. Jonathan's dedication paid off, however. He soon received offers to model clothes for store catalogs and newspaper and magazine advertisements. One modeling job led to another. But simply standing still and posing was not the same as acting. The youngster knew he still had a long way to go.

Jonathan got his first chance to display his acting ability with a local theater group. In a holiday production of *Scrooge* at the Chatauqua Theater in Sacramento, he played two roles—the young Scrooge and Tiny Tim. Jonathan really enjoyed performing on stage. The audiences also enjoyed his work, and he received excellent reviews.

In addition to his acting ability, Jonathan also had a distinctive voice which set him apart from other boys his age. Although Jonathan claims it is "just an ordinary kid's voice," it has an unusual gravelly quality to it. His voice got Jonathan assignments doing voice-overs, in which the speaker is not seen on screen. Jonathan became the voice of several cartoon characters and even did a voice-over for a Japanese commercial. He was getting valuable experience, and each part gave him another item to add to his credits.

To learn even more about show business, Jonathan and his mom attended a seminar given by Hollywood talent manager Gary Scalzo. Scalzo convinced them that he could help the talented youngster achieve his dream. But Jonathan would have to move to Los Angeles. Jonathan had made great strides in one year, but if he was going to get to the next level, this was a logical step. His mother was behind him all the way, and she agreed to move to Los Angeles with him. Jonathan's brother and father remained behind in Sacramento.

The other young talents who caught the agent's eye were set up in an apartment complex in Hollywood. Here they could give support to one another as they worked toward their common goal. Among those who lived in this little community were Angela Watson (*Step by Step*), Carol-Ann Plante (*Harry and the Hendersons*), and Elijah Wood (*The Good Son*). Soon Jonathan signed with the agency Helfond, Joseph and Rix, which promptly sent him out on auditions.

Jonathan prospered in his new surroundings. He enjoyed every aspect of the actor's life, including the endless readings and auditions. Within weeks of his move, he landed his first national commercial for Burger King. Others for Kellogg's Product 19, Mattel Toys, and various regional products followed in rapid succession.

Around this time, Jonathan landed his first role in a movie. It was only an industrial film, however, and was not released to the public. Nevertheless, as a working actor, Jonathan now became a member of the Screen Actors Guild (SAG), a necessity for all those who appear on camera.

Playing the role of Kevin Brady, Jonathan enjoys a laugh with his television father in a scene from the CBS series The Bradys. *The show was excellent experience for Jonathan, who quickly learned to work with other actors, take direction, deliver lines, and create a character.*

Jonathan could not use his full name, however. Another actor was already registered under Jonathan Taylor Weiss, and Guild rules forbid more than one person from using the exact same name. So Jonathan took Jonathan Taylor Thomas as his screen name. Thomas is the middle name of his brother, Joel.

Despite his success, finances were a problem. National commercials paid well, but bills had a way of piling up. Rent, food, and clothes for auditions cost money. Whenever possible, Jonathan and his mother traveled to Sacramento to be with their family. These trips were important since they gave him a chance to return to his regular school and see his friends, but they also were costly.

Then one day in early 1990, Jonathan auditioned for a part in a new CBS television series called *The Bradys*, a follow-up series to the popular *Brady Bunch* show of the 1970s. *The Bradys* was going to follow the lives of the kids from the earlier series, kids who now had families of their own. The role Jonathan tried out for was that of Kevin Brady, son of Greg, the oldest child in the original show.

To Jonathan's delight, he got the part of Kevin. The young actor had a role in a new network series. His dream of appearing on TV was coming true. Had Jonathan not won the role, it is uncertain how long he and his mother would have been able to continue with their demanding schedule.

Jonathan loved his new work. *The Bradys* debuted that February and all seemed right in the youngster's world.

But things do not always go according to plan. Viewers did not enjoy *The Bradys* as much as the network had hoped. Just as Jonathan was getting used to life as a television actor, the show was canceled. Only seven episodes were aired. Suddenly, his dream had come to a screeching halt.

Luckily for Jonathan, new opportunities have a way of presenting themselves. A couple of months after *The Bradys* went off the air, Jonathan auditioned for another new show called *Hammer Time*, which was to star stand-up comedian Tim Allen. *Hammer Time* would forever change young Jonathan Taylor Thomas's life.

4

HOME IMPROVEMENT

Hammer Time was created as a sitcom especially for comedian Tim Allen. Since starting out in show business, Allen had developed the stage character of a manly, tool-loving, Mr. Fix-It-type fellow, known for his trademark grunt of "Aaarrgh! Aaarrgh!" The show placed his character in a family setting, in which he plays the part of Tim Taylor, host of a cable TV home-improvement program. He is assisted on the show by Al Borland, played by Richard Karn. Tim is kind of a poor man's Bob Vila, who has a similar real-life show. The main difference between Tim and Vila is that Tim's projects more often than not wind up in a puff of smoke. Al usually has to bail him out with his know-how. At home, Tim's wife, Jill, played by Patricia Richardson, keeps the family running smoothly as she oversees the couple's three sons, Brad, Randy, and Mark, and works outside the home.

Jonathan won the role of Randy Taylor, the wise-cracking, studious, middle son, beating out 750 other actors for the part. In his favor was the fact that some who were casting the series felt Jonathan strongly resembled Tim Allen. The young actor still had to outperform the others, however,

Jonathan (seated), surrounded by his TV family from Home Improvement, *looks every bit the part of the mischief-making middle son, Randy, the role that made him a TV star.*

and that he did. During the third round of auditions, one network executive reportedly said, "That kid's gonna be a star."

As Jonathan describes Randy: "He has two parents and a very loving home. He realizes he's secure, but he's still insecure in a way. He feels he *has* to joke around. That's how he relates to people. He's also a huge con artist. He's always getting into mischief, his wheels are always turning." Jonathan admits that there is a lot of himself in Randy. "I think we're alike," he says, "because I also get into mischief, but I'm a good kid. I'm also a good student, but I do like to scheme. I'm always thinking about the next thing I can do—but I would never take things to the extent that Randy does."

Brad, the oldest son, is played by Zachery Ty Bryan. Zachery is actually a month younger than Jonathan, though he is several inches taller. Brad is athletic but takes a backseat to Randy when it comes to schoolwork. Together, the two spend a major part of their time tormenting their younger brother, Mark. Played by Taran Noah Smith, Mark idolizes his father and usually believes everything he is told.

In addition to his family, Tim also has a neighbor, Wilson Wilson, the never-completely-seen voice of reason. Wilson, played by Earl Hindman, always manages to have a portion of his face hidden, whether it be by a fence, lamp, coffeepot, or snowman. Whenever Tim needs advice, he seeks out Wilson, who often counsels him by quoting long-dead philosophers.

By the time the new series filmed the pilot episode, its name had been changed to *Tool Time*. The show was picked up by ABC, and the actors signed standard seven-year contracts, although the seven years were not guaranteed. Only the popularity of the show would determine if it lasted past its initial season.

Before it made its debut in the fall of 1991, however, the show's title was changed once again. *Tool Time* remained the name of Tim Taylor's cable program while the ABC series officially became *Home Improvement*.

Nothing is sure in television, and there was always the possibility that *Home Improvement* would fail, as did *The Bradys*. Nevertheless, Jonathan and his mother and brother decided it was time to make a permanent move. Jonathan's parents had been having marital problems and had separated in 1990; by 1991 they had divorced. Jonathan's father continued to live in Sacramento while the rest of the family packed their belongings and moved to the San Fernando Valley, not far from Hollywood.

On Tuesday, September 17, 1991, *Home Improvement* made its network debut. It was given the spot between two of ABC's hit comedies, *Full House* and *Roseanne* (one of Jonathan's favorite shows). The show proved to be an immediate hit, and by the end of the season, it was the top new show on TV. Tim Allen's star quality and the show's family-oriented appeal combined to make it a favorite with viewers of all ages. It won the 1992 People's Choice Award in the Favorite New Comedy Series category and was also nominated for an Emmy by the

On-screen, Tim Allen and Jonathan share a father-son relationship. Offscreen, they developed an especially close bond, as Jonathan looked to Tim as a mentor and teacher.

Academy of Television Arts and Sciences. An Emmy is the most prestigious award a show, or an individual TV performer, can win.

The three boys helped make the new show popular with younger viewers. Jonathan, who had just turned 10 shortly before the show's debut, developed a special relationship with Tim Allen. The boy's parents were divorced, so he did not see much of his father. Tim's father had been killed by a drunk driver when Tim was 11. Added to that common bond was the similarity in their personalities. Each was outgoing and used humor to get them past life's daily obstacles.

Jonathan looked up to Tim, watching him intently at all times. He learned a great deal by observing how Tim went about his daily business. The older actor was always cracking jokes and cutting up on the set. When it was time for work, however, he stopped clowning around and performed as a true professional.

"Tim keeps everybody loose on the set," says Jonathan. "You can threaten Tim with the worst of things, and he'll still turn it into a joke. He's amazing, but at the same time, very professional, gets his work done. He's the loosest, mellowest guy you'll ever know—a blast to work with."

Jonathan's mom appreciated the interest Tim showed in her son. "Tim Allen is a big help," she said. "He keeps an eye on Jonathan and takes a special interest. Tim knows that Jonathan's dad and I are divorced, and his dad, who lives in Sacramento, doesn't see him a lot. Tim helps keep Jonathan's head from swelling. If he sees any ego flaring, he playfully teases Jonathan."

Much as Jonathan enjoyed his work on the show, he still looked forward to hanging out with his friends when work was over. Unfortunately, the schedule of an actor in a regular TV show does not leave a lot of free time for other things. *Home Improvement*'s schedule was three weeks work followed by one week off. Taping ran from late July, when it first began, until April, when production stopped for the season. Jonathan's day, which by law had to include three hours of schooling by a tutor, began at the studio by 9:00 A.M. From Monday through Thursday, he was finished by 6:00 P.M. On Fridays, however, when the show was actually taped, he was usually not through until later.

The second season of *Home Improvement* picked up where the first had left off. The show became even more of a favorite, despite a switch to Wednesday evenings. Again it won a People's Choice Award, this time for Favorite Comedy Series, and was also nominated for five Emmy Awards. *Home Improvement's* success was reflected in its showing in the Nielsen ratings. The Nielsen ratings provide an estimate of the size of the audience which watches every television show. After *Home Improvement's* first season, it finished fifth on the charts with a rating of 17.5. That meant that an average of 17.5 percent of all households which had TV sets tuned in to the program. By the end of the 1992-1993 season, it had moved up two positions to finish at number three with a rating of 19.2 percent.

ABC was so happy with the show's performance that in an extremely unusual move, the network renewed *Home Improvement* for three years. It was a strong display of confidence for everyone involved with the show.

Jonathan did not just sit back and rest on his laurels, however. Rather than take the next couple of months off, he made guest appearances on several TV specials. In addition, he continued doing his voice-over work for cartoons and commercials. As *Home Improvement's* popularity increased, so too did Jonathan's. His wholesome good looks and pleasant personality won him more and

The incredible popularity of Home Improvement *was explained by Tim Allen, here with Jonathan and costar, Patricia Richardson, when he said it was because of the chemistry between the cast members.*

Jonathan, at front and center, shares the stage with the cast of Home Improvement *at the 1993 People's Choice Awards, where the show won for Favorite Comedy Series.*

more fans. Despite his growing success, he never forgot the lessons his mother taught him while growing up. He always remembered that other people were just as important as he was. Jonathan became involved with several charities, donating much of his time to helping bring smiles to the faces of others.

Season number three for *Home Improvement* saw the show's popularity continue to climb. It began, however, on a somewhat sour note. The three "brothers" did not show up for work on the first day they were due on the set. The story which appeared in print was that the boys were on strike, looking for big raises in their salaries and other additional benefits. The three were depicted as ungrateful, and *Home Improvement* was reportedly ready to fire the youngsters and begin auditioning new actors for their parts.

The real story had more to do with safety and health concerns, although the boys' agents undoubtedly did feel that their clients deserved more money. Matters were eventually settled. Jonathan, Zachery, and Taran returned to the set, and the show picked up where it had left off without missing a beat.

As the boys grew older, their characters developed more and more. Young and old alike tuned in each week to see what new antics the brothers got involved in and how Tim's ineptitude and clumsiness would reach new heights. By the time the season ended, the show had attained the top spot in the Nielsen ratings. With 21.8 percent of the audience viewing it each week, *Home Improvement* was the most-watched program on TV for the 1993-1994 season. As such, it gave ABC its first top-rated show since *Roseanne* four years earlier.

As part of the best-loved TV show in the country, Jonathan was ready to take the next big step in his show-business career. He was ready to break into movies.

5

THE BOY WHO WOULD
BE LION KING

Disney was putting together a star-studded cast of voices for its new animated feature, *The Lion King*. The company had already signed James Earl Jones, Matthew Broderick, Whoopi Goldberg, Jeremy Irons, and Cheech Marin as the voices for some of the characters. One of the roles which remained to be filled was that of Simba, the young lion cub who is the pivotal character.

For Jonathan, the unique "raspy" quality of his voice was his ticket to success on the big screen. Producer Don Hahn recalls: "We had this role for a scrappy young kid to play Simba, and we looked at dozens and dozens of actors . . . We saw [Jonathan] on *Home Improvement* and just thought his voice was right. It gives him a very distinctive character."

Much to his surprise, the role went to Jonathan. "I didn't expect ever in a million years to be doing TV *and* movies," said the youngster. The character of Simba was very similar to that of Randy on *Home Improvement*. As Jonathan noted, "Simba and Randy are both curious kids, they're both intuitive and confident, always ready to throw that fast one in, that little comment."

Because Jonathan's role of Simba was spread out over

Jonathan's voice-over training and, more importantly, his unique voice, won him the speaking role of the lion cub Simba in Disney's animated megahit, The Lion King.

the course of nearly two years, his voice had to be at its strongest. He did special exercises to strengthen it and had to be careful not to accidentally damage his vocal chords by yelling. In most of Jonathan's other roles, he worked together with a cast. For *The Lion King*, he performed alone in a soundproof booth, which presented a real challenge. As he explained: "I was in there in a room alone, and I not only had to play my character, but [also] the people I was talking to. I had to get inside their heads so I would know what Simba would be reacting to."

The role also turned out to be quite physical. "We darn near beat him up when we were recording," Hahn told *People* magazine. "We had to make it sound like he was being flung down chutes in the elephant graveyard and being chased by wildebeests. So we would rough him up at the microphone and try to make him out of breath."

When the animators took over, they tried to incorporate Jonathan's facial and body expressions into the character of Simba. They were incredibly successful. "When I saw the movie with my mother," said Jonathan, "she said, 'That's what you do when you get sad. That's what you do when you're happy.' It's pretty cool to be immortalized in a Disney classic."

Since it was a Disney production, hopes were high for *The Lion King*. Everyone was reasonably certain that it would follow down the path set by other recent Disney animated hits. However, no one, realistically, could have expected it to be as big a hit as it was.

The Lion King opened in Hollywood on June 17, 1994. When the first reviews came out in

The smile of the cub Simba seems to bear a remarkable resemblance to Jonathan's infectious grin. While delighted to do the speaking role, Jonathan refused to sing for Simba, protesting that he could in no way carry a tune.

the newspapers, it was apparent that *The Lion King* had the potential to be a record-breaker. On its opening weekend, the film grossed an incredible $42 million. By the end of 1994, *The Lion King* had brought in more than $750 million at box offices around the world. It did not just make more money than any animated film ever—it made more than *any* film ever did in a single year at that time.

As was to be expected with such a smash hit, *The Lion King* won many awards, including Golden Globe Awards for Best Musical Comedy Film and Best Original Song, as well a Grammy nomination for Best Song of the Year. The film also won Academy Award Oscars for Best Original Score and Best Original Song. Best of all for Jonathan were the excellent reviews he received for his role. He was now more in demand than ever before. The future was looking even brighter for the up-and-coming young star.

6

LIGHTS, CAMERA, ACTION!

Jonathan had actually received offers to appear in movies before *The Lion King* came along. He was unable to accept them because of his busy schedule and his commitment to *Home Improvement*. Following the show's third season, however, he was offered a part in a new live-action Disney film that was to be shot during the summer break before the new season began.

The film, which starred Chevy Chase and Farrah Fawcett, was to be called *Man-2-Man*. In it, Jonathan plays Farrah's son, Ben Archer, who has been the "man of the house" since his father left them. When his mother becomes involved with a new boyfriend (Chevy Chase), Ben feels threatened and tries to drive him away.

The film was to be shot in Vancouver, Canada. Jonathan and his mother, who by this time was acting as his manager so she could spend more time with him and help him make decisions, decided this role was one he could accept. "There's a lot of laughs," said Jonathan, "but there are a lot of dramatic, real-life issues, too." In an interview, Jonathan explained his character: "It's not him being a bad kid. He's protecting the most important

---

From the small screen to the big screen was Jonathan's goal. He reached that goal when he made his first on-screen appearance in a major feature film, Man of the House.

39

thing in his life." He confided, "Ben came from a single-parent home and I grew up in a single-parent home. I think that in itself was dramatic."

James Orr, the director of the movie, was impressed with Jonathan's ability and professionalism. "I wanted a young actor who had the soul of a poet, because everything Ben does comes from vulnerability, fear, and insecurity, not from any meanness or inherent negative qualities," said Orr. He continued, "Jonathan is very three-dimensional. He's an extraordinary person and very talented. I've rarely met a twelve year old who impresses me as much as he does." In another interview, Orr commented, "He radiates this intelligence and dimension, and not only does he have this great comic timing, but he has this depth of emotion."

Since the film was shot in Canada, it gave Jonathan a chance to experience brand new surroundings in another country. He enjoyed traveling and was awed by the natural beauty of the Vancouver region. The location also gave him a chance to partake in his favorite hobby— fishing. "The movie crew flew us over to Vancouver Island to go fishing," he said. "We went salmon fishing five times. . . ."

Jonathan finished shooting shortly before he was due back to work at *Home Improvement*. In the meantime, the movie had been retitled *Man of the House*. The movie opened on March 3, 1995. It received mixed reviews but was still the top-grossing film in its first week of release. Jonathan received a great deal of the credit for its success. *Daily Variety* wrote: "Jonathan Taylor Thomas was the 'man' of the box office

as Disney's *Man of the House* led the week-end with an estimated $9.2 million. Chevy Chase and Farrah Fawcett may be *back* in the *Man of the House*, but it's the young *Home Improvement* costar who's receiving credit for the comedy's opening momentum." *Entertainment Weekly* stated: "Who gets the credit for *Man of the House*'s posing a solid $9.5 million to become the weekend's first place finisher? As with the stepfather/son relationship in the film, the edge goes to

Jonathan, seen here with director James Orr on location for Man of the House, *was a great hit with the cast of the film, all of whom were impressed with the profession-alism of the 12-year-old actor.*

Jonathan Taylor Thomas. Following the lead of his *Home Improvement* dad, Tim Allen, Thomas could parlay his sitcom role into a big-screen career."

In *Home Improvement's* fourth season, Randy met his first girlfriend. Just as his character was developing this new relationship on the show, Jonathan's relationship with his TV brothers was changing in real life. Zachery began to drift away from Jonathan and became closer to Taran. The breach was mostly because of the boys' changing interests. It may also have been, in part, the result of Jonathan's new status as a movie celebrity. He was receiving much more fan mail than the others. It was only natural that the other boys might feel they were no longer on equal terms with Jonathan.

Jonathan accepted the break and tried to handle the matter in a mature fashion. "People are going to change," he acknowledged, "and they're gonna have their differences, and those differences are gonna be there for a long, long time." However, he insists, ". . . we *do* get along, and that shows on the show. I think we have a very good chemistry on the set, and it's reflected in the outcome of the show."

Jonathan was rapidly becoming one of the most sought-after young actors in Hollywood. Before *Home Improvement's* fourth season had even finished, he had already signed on to shoot another movie. *Tom and Huck*, to be filmed in Huntsville, Alabama, was based on Mark Twain's classic book, *The Adventures of Tom Sawyer*.

Tom and Huck was the first time that Jonathan was the headlining star of the film

right from the start. He admitted, "Of all the characters I've played, I'm probably the most like Tom Sawyer—adventurous. I don't know if I'm so precocious as Tom Sawyer is; he is pretty conniving. But we're both active and have a sneaky side to us."

Jonathan's role as Tom gave him the opportunity to visit another part of the country. At the same time, he had a chance to learn about a different time in our nation's history. This appealed to Jonathan, who counts history as

As Tom Sawyer in Tom and Huck, Jonathan displays a sly smile as his friends do his work for him. His keen interest in learning more about America's past made this "period piece" film especially enjoyable for Jonathan.

one of his favorite subjects in school. As he told a reporter: "I think it's cool doing a period piece. . . . I think it'll give me a good background of what it was like to live back then, because the director was telling me he wants to make it very authentic." Ironically, school became associated with the movie in another way. Jonathan had to take his final exams for seventh grade while sitting in the back of a cave on the set of the film.

Director Peter Hewitt was also impressed with his young star. "He absorbs what's going on like a sponge," said Hewitt. "I could very easily see him moving into directing, if that's what he would wish."

Tom and Huck relates the adventures of Tom Sawyer and his friends Huck Finn (Brad Renfro) and Becky Thatcher (Rachael Leigh Cook). Their adventures involve murder, buried treasure, and their travels down the Mississippi River. Over the course of the film, Jonathan experienced another big moment in his life—his first on-screen kiss.

Jonathan's next film opportunity presented itself in short order. No sooner had *Tom and Huck* finished filming than *The Adventures of Pinocchio* was scheduled to go into production. *Pinocchio*, of course, is the classic children's story written in 1883 by Carlo Collodi. The tale revolves around Geppetto, an old puppet maker who carves the puppet Pinocchio, who then comes to life. The updated version combined live action, animation, and animatronics. The movie starred Academy Award-winner Martin Landau as Geppetto.

"Getting to work with Martin Landau was great," reported Jonathan. "He's done over 75

In The Adventures of Pinocchio, *Jonathan combined the role of the "real" boy and the voice of the puppet. Pinocchio was a computer-generated puppet that was actually drawn in Jonathan's image.*

Working with Martin Landau, Jonathan's costar in Pinocchio, *was a thrill for the young actor who greatly admires the veteran performer.*

films and numerous plays. He's a very fine man, one of the few teaching actors out there. I learned a lot by watching him and being with him . . ." Jonathan's costars were Rob Schneider, Udo Kier, and Bebe Neuwirth. The film was shot just outside Prague in the Czech Republic, which gave Jonathan another chance to explore a different part of the world.

Part of the fun of *The Adventures of Pinocchio* is seeing how the live action, animation, and animatronics are blended together. "I think that the puppet does look like me," said Jonathan. "People are going to see this movie and go, 'How on earth did they do this?' The puppet not only has big expressions, but it does subtle things and throughout the film, you get close to this puppet. And you know, you forget that this thing isn't real."

The Adventures of Pinocchio was released in July of 1996, shortly after *Home Improvement* completed its fifth hit season. Before it was even released, Jonathan was already busy at work filming *Wild America*, a movie that would prove to be one of his personal favorites.

Shot in Atlanta, Georgia, and Alberta, Canada, *Wild America* is based on the true adventures of the three Stouffer brothers, Marty, Mark, and Marshall. The brothers began making nature films while in their teens and later produced the PBS series *Wild America*. Set in the summer of 1967, the movie follows the brothers as they travel across the country in search of wildlife. The parts of the two older brothers are played by Scott Bairstow and Devon Sawa.

Wild America was Jonathan's first "star vehicle." The film is related through the eyes of the youngest brother, Marshall, played by Jonathan. Director William Dear left no doubt as to Jonathan's importance to the production. "He is the linchpin of the movie," said Dear, "the name who could get the movie made."

Those involved with the film got a glimpse of Jonathan's immense popularity during the shooting. "We were there maybe two and a half

The film Wild America *is especially dear to Jonathan's heart because of his avid support of environmental and wildlife causes. Although the film was not a great box-office hit, Jonathan is proud to have brought the issues to people's attention.*

hours," reported Dear. "There was nobody around when we started [shooting]—it wasn't a spot you could necessarily walk to—and by the time we finished, there must have been forty or fifty girls hanging around. That's what happens when you're shooting on location with a teen idol." Says Linda Kay, president of the National Association of Fan Clubs, "He's the most popular teenage star consistently over the past four or five years."

The movie became a special job for Jonathan. "I love animals," he told one reporter. "I love wildlife. I'm a big supporter, although I haven't studied it. For me to get to work with these animals was great." To another he said: "I think we all have an affinity with animals. I think working this closely gives you a greater appreciation and more respect for them. . . . When you see the power and magic that most animals have, you start wanting to preserve that for future generations."

The film was released in the summer of 1997. The *San Francisco Chronicle* called it ". . . a terrific new film with a simple calling card: old-fashioned adventure with down-to-earth characters. It's been a while since Hollywood turned out anything as likable." It continues, "The film is sharp thrills and delightful fun with a thoroughly engaging cast headed by Jonathan Taylor Thomas . . ."

Unfortunately, not everyone else agreed. The movie was a disappointment at the box office. It was not enough, however, to derail Jonathan's career. As Hollywood agent Judy Savage put it: "Generally, kids who are really successful in Hollywood are small for their age and have kind of a pleasant, blendable look; they don't have to be gorgeous. The ones who succeed are generally very smart, and the luck comes in when they're in a project that takes off, whether it's a hit television series or a movie that makes a lot of money. Jonathan Taylor Thomas has the whole package. He's got a darling voice, plus he's smart, adorable and talented."

A combination like that is hard to beat.

7

THE LIFE OF A STAR

Like any other person in any other business, Jonathan has a life of his own when he is not in front of the cameras. Away from work, he spends time with his family, in school, with charities, enjoying his hobbies, and being with his friends.

As far as Jonathan is concerned, his family always comes first. Since his parents divorced, his mother, Claudine, has been the most important person in his life. As he told *USA Today*, his mother is his hero because of her "incredible strength and integrity. . . . She's a great friend. A great mom. A great business partner. She's really everything."

Jonathan has a typical brother relationship with his older sibling, Joel. They both enjoy playing basketball, but Jonathan usually comes up short. Joel, you see, was a standout guard at Agoura High School. He also starred on the school's football team as an end, and continues to excel in college.

Although there is the normal amount of brotherly rivalry between the two, Jonathan knows he can count on Joel when he needs help with homework, or even just some advice.

Although a star, Jonathan does not allow his career to come before his family, friends, his education, or the many charitable causes to which he gives so much of his time and effort.

One time, for example, Jonathan was being urged by his friends at school to ask out a girl who was a good friend. Not sure of what to do, he turned to Joel.

"I asked my brother, 'What do you think we should do?'" said Jonathan. "My brother told me it was up to me and said to just make sure you stay friends, no matter what."

As you can imagine, it's extremely hard to juggle a full-time job and school at the same time. Jonathan, however, has proven that he can do anything he puts his mind to. He has maintained an A average throughout his school years while splitting time between work and studies. As far as the benefits of a classroom compared to a tutor, Jonathan prefers the tutor. "With the tutor," he explains, "you get more undivided attention, versus a class with thirty kids."

Jonathan's favorite academic subjects include history, English, and science. Like many other youngsters, he counts math among his least favorites. "It's not that I don't like it," he explains, "it's just that it's time consuming. It's just frustrating, 'cause it takes so much time to do."

It is easy to see how Jonathan's busy schedule can seem overwhelming at times. "I get tired of working long hours," he says. "And doing a lot of night shooting and traveling, you get tired. But I have fun, too, and that's how you learn. There are times that you want to relax and be able to chill out. But I do get those times, and you have to take advantage of the few breaks that come along."

When he does have free time, he likes to relax with his hobbies. He enjoys sports of all kinds, especially soccer, basketball, skiing, and roller-hockey. He carries a small scar on his forehead as a result of a high-sticking accident during a roller-hockey game. Unfortunately, his schedule does not allow him to participate in organized leagues as much as he would like. As far as professional sports teams go, he's a big fan of the New York Mets in baseball, the Boston Celtics in basketball, and the Chicago Bears in football.

The hobby which takes up most of his spare time, however, is fishing. Jonathan is always buying new gear in anticipation of his next fishing excursion. The hobby allows him the opportunity to relax and get in touch with nature, away from the hectic day-to-day life of an actor. When he was asked by a reporter what his favorite childhood memory was, the answer was easy. "Going fishing in Alaska with my Grampa and mom," he replied, "and catching two sixty-five-pound halibut!"

As you would probably expect from someone so academically inclined, Jonathan also loves to read. He spends time on his computer (he has an official web page on the Celebrity Sightings Internet site). "I still like traditional reading," Jonathan told *People* magazine, "but I also like sitting at the computer and opening up a book. I've got Encarta, an encyclopedia on CD-ROM, that I use when I'm writing reports." He also enjoys listening to music (his favorite artists include Boyz II Men, the Dave Matthews Band, Shai, and Silk) and collecting sports cards, autographs, and hats.

And of course, Jonathan also loves animals. His family has three pets—a Lhasa apso, a Himalayan cat named Simba, and Simba's mother, Sami (short for Samantha). Just because he's famous, it doesn't mean he gets away with not doing chores around the house. "Every night," says Jonathan, "I have to clean the cat-litter box, and clean my animals' dishes, and let my dog out, and feed my cat and dog."

Jonathan has a special soft spot in his heart for those charities which deal with children. He has participated in fund raisers for Michael Jackson's Heal the World organization and has given time to the Children's Miracle Network, the Boy Scouts of America, Ronald McDonald House, the annual Sail with the Stars Cruise, and Famous Fone Friends. About his work to benefit Phoenix Children's Hospital's Emily Anderson Family Learning Center, Jonathan told one newspaper reporter: "It's important to give back. Everyone has to deal with illness at some time in their life. We just want to tell the children we understand what they are going through and hope we can make their day a little happier."

Fans are also important to Jonathan. One of his greatest disappointments is that he is unable to personally respond to the thousands of letters he receives. "If there's one thing I could do besides making a better world," he says, "it would be to write back more. I get swamped with fan letters, and I do read them. I appreciate each and every letter. I feel bad that kids take the time and effort to write stuff that comes from deep down in their hearts. It's real important stuff. I'd love to sit down and write a two-page letter to each one, and if I had the time, believe me, I would." Since this obviously isn't possible, Jonathan tries to do what he can in other ways. He takes part in autograph

For Jonathan, the "right" girl will have to share his values, which were instilled in him by his mother. Claudine taught Jonathan the importance of generosity and giving, and the lessons have stayed with the young man throughout his career.

sessions all over the country as often as he can.

Many of the letters Jonathan receives come from female fans pledging their love to him. But what does Jonathan look for in a person? That's easy. Someone who is easy to talk to and who cares about others. Someone who is not impressed with him for being a celebrity but who likes him for himself. Jonathan says he looks for "someone who is nice and intelligent and likes to do things that are rugged—like hiking in the mountains—but at the same time can enjoy theater or music and museums."

Jonathan sees himself with a wife in the future, one or two kids, and several family pets. He would like to live in the mountains, where he could fish and hike to his heart's content. At the same time, it is important to him that his home be in "a safe place for my family to grow up." He has also said he may someday return to the East Coast, where he was born in Pennsylvania. The future looks bright, indeed, for young Jonathan Taylor Thomas.

With college looming on the horizon, Jonathan did not work on any films during *Home Improvement*'s 1997 summer break. Instead, he decided to concentrate on his studies, which included a long, required summer-reading list. As Jonathan said: "I'm trying not to procrastinate on my reading. I won't have the luxury, when doing film or television, of finishing a shot and then going back to my trailer for a half an hour. I have to study or knock off ten or fifteen math problems before I go back to work."

In the fall of 1997, *Home Improvement* began its seventh season on ABC. Rumors made the rounds that it would be the show's last season. By the spring of 1998, however, the show's star, Tim Allen, revealed that it would continue for another year. In August of 1998, it was announced that Jonathan would leave *Home Improvement* early in the 1998-99 season to devote more time to his studies.

Jonathan's movie career is not as uncertain. The release of Disney's romantic comedy *I'll Be Home for Christmas* was scheduled for the 1998 holiday season. In it, Jonathan plays a young man who attends a prep school in California. His father offers him a new Porsche if he will come back east for the Christmas holidays. He decides to go, but along the way gets dumped in the desert with no money. While all this is happening, he's also trying to keep his girlfriend (played by Jessica Biel of TV's *7th Heaven*) from falling in love with another guy. In Jonathan's own words, "It's kind of like 'Ferris Bueller's Day Off' meets 'Trains, Planes and Automobiles' meets 'The Sure Thing.'"

Although unconfirmed, Jonathan's next film project reportedly will be *The Life of Bruce Henry*, the inspirational true story of a Maine man who is fighting to overcome Lou Gehrig's disease (amyotrophic lateral sclerosis) and Parkinson's disease. He has struggled to beat these two neuromuscular diseases and has helped to raise money for various charities. Jonathan has been cast to play Henry as a young man, and Gary Busey will play him as an adult. The movie is tentatively scheduled for release in the year 2000.

What does Jonathan see in the way of future roles? As he told a reporter for *USA Today*, he sometimes feels like he's being pulled every which way. "The studios want you to do very, very, very edgy, artistic, sometimes violent films which seem to be the trend these days and then you have the obligation to the fans and the viewers who are younger. And you want to do something for families because family films are slowly dying."

In a change of pace, Jonathan has also taken part in another project, this one to help the STARBRIGHT Foundation, a nonprofit organization headed by Chairman Steven Spielberg and Capital Campaign Chairman General Norman Schwarzkopf. The foundation raises money to help seriously ill children, an important cause to Jonathan.

STARBRIGHT, together with a book company, is publishing *The Emperor's New Clothes: An All-Star Illustrated Retelling of the Classic Fairy Tale*. It will take the form of a book and CD

Jonathan truly enjoys meeting as many of his fans as possible and signing autographs. Often, he runs behind schedule to make sure that everyone gets an autograph or has a chance to shake his hand or take a photograph with him.

package due to be released in October 1998. Hans Christian Andersen's classic tale has been rewritten by a collection of today's most popular celebrities, each of whom wrote a chapter from the point of view of a character in the original story or from that of a new character. Jonathan tells his chapter from the perspective of the emperor's teenage son. Others who donated their time and energy to the project include Jay Leno, Liam Neeson, Harrison Ford, Melissa Mathison, Rita Wilson, Angela Lansbury, Nathan Lane, Jason Alexander, Dr. Ruth Westheimer, Madonna, Penny Marshall, Carrie Fisher, Melissa Joan Hart, Jeff Goldblum, Dan Aykroyd, Robin Williams, Geena Davis, Calvin Klein, Rosie

O'Donnell, Fran Drescher, Joan Rivers, General Schwarzkopf, and John Lithgow.

Show business is not the only thing on Jonathan's mind, nor has it ever been. His schoolwork continues to be a top priority. While in Canada shooting *I'll Be Home for Christmas*, Jonathan took time out to take the SAT exam at a Vancouver high school. His plans for the future definitely involve college. He intends to make sure he has something to fall back on in case he decides to stop acting. "I'm trying to get the best education I can," he says. "You know, you've seen it a million times where kids are doing extremely well in this business, careers are looking great, then the next day you don't hear about them anymore. . . . I don't know if I'll be able to fit films in with college. Put it this way: College would never not happen because of a film. Films might not happen because of college." Jonathan is currently thinking of attending either Yale University or Northwestern University. While in college, he likely will study some aspect of the film industry.

Jonathan currently seems to be leaning toward a career behind the cameras, possibly in directing, writing, or producing. He counts Jodie Foster and Ron Howard as people in the business whom he admires for the way they have been able to make their marks in the entertainment industry after having been successful child actors.

However, Jonathan does not rule out a different field altogether—that of politics. He watches C-Span on television every night and keeps up with what is happening in the news. He is especially concerned with things that affect our environment. As he puts it, "Generations to come, they're not going to have forests and streams and meadows. Not if we keep doing what we're doing, polluting and destroying animal habitats. It's just wrong."

Speaking during a Celebrity Sightings chat, he said, "I may be just naive, but I don't know, I'd like to be in politics, but I'd like to be in honest politics and direct politics. I'm not interested in the political game, I'm more into just straight out, bare bones politics, making differences, making changes and getting things done, being effective."

Being around adults all the time has undoubtedly given him a more mature attitude than most people his age. "I just think that the adult world is very interesting," says Jonathan. "I like talking to adults because they've had so many more experiences than kids have had, and you can learn a lot from them. That's one thing that kids take for granted. When you're around adults, you should learn what you can. They've been around a lot more than us, and they can tell you a lot."

Jonathan is determined not to make the same mistakes made by many young stars. "I've made a point not to make [acting] my whole life," he says. "There are other sides to my personality and other sides to my life. If this business went away, it would be a blow, because I've put a lot into it. But it wouldn't be devastating because I have an education."

With an attitude like that, Jonathan Taylor Thomas will be successful in whatever direction he decides to go. Of that, you can be certain.

CHRONOLOGY

1981   Jonathan Taylor Weiss is born on September 8, 1981, in Bethlehem, Pennsylvania.

1986   Weiss family moves to Sacramento, California.

1988   Jonathan signs with Grimme Talent agency.

1990   Jonathan wins role of Kevin Brady in *The Bradys* TV series, which airs from February through March; around this time, he changes his name to Jonathan Taylor Thomas.

1991   Jonathan's parents, Stephen and Claudine Weiss, divorce; Jonathan wins role of Randy Taylor in *Home Improvement*; in September, *Home Improvement* makes debut on ABC.

1994   *The Lion King* is released.

1995   *Man of the House* is released; *Tom and Huck* is released.

1996   *The Adventures of Pinocchio* is released.

1997   *Wild America* is released.

1998   Jonathan wins award as Nickelodeon Kids' Choice Favorite Television Actor for role in *Home Improvement*; it is announced that he will leave the show during the 1998-99 season; *I'll Be Home for Christmas* to be released for the 1998 holiday season.

ACCOMPLISHMENTS

Feature Films

1994   *The Lion King* (voice)

1995   *Man of the House*
        Tom and Huck

1996   *The Adventures of Pinocchio*

1997   *Wild America*

1998   *I'll Be Home for Christmas*

Videos

1996   *Who Stole Santa?* (voice)
        Christmas in Oz (voice)
        Toto Lost in New York (voice)
        The Nome Prince and the Magic Belt (voice)
        The Oz Kids (voice)

Television

1990   *The Bradys*
        In Living Color (guest appearance)

1991–98 *Home Improvement*

1992   *A Busch Gardens—Sea World Summer Safari*

1994   *The Making of The Lion King*

1995   *Behind Closed Doors with Joan Lunden*

1995   *America's Funniest Home Videos* (guest appearance)

FURTHER READING

Elias, Justine. "A Teen Idol Outgrowing His Image." *The New York Times*, June 27, 1997.

Johns, Michael-Anne. *Totally JTT*. New York: Pocket Books, Simon & Schuster, Inc., 1996.

"The Jonathan Taylor Thomas Life Story!" *Teen Beat*, October 1995.

"Jonathan Taylor Thomas Is Totally Yours." *BOP* magazine, 1998.

"Just When You Thought You Knew Everything About JTT." *BOP* magazine,

ABOUT THE AUTHOR

John F. Grabowski is a native of Brooklyn, New York. He holds a bachelor's degree in psychology from City College of New York and a master's degree in educational psychology from Teacher's College, Columbia University. He has been a teacher for 29 years, as well as a freelance writer, specializing in the fields of sports, education, and comedy. His body of published work includes 18 books; a nationally syndicated sports column; consultation on several math textbooks; articles for newspapers, magazines, and the programs of professional sports teams; and comedy material sold to Jay Leno, Joan Rivers, and numerous other comics. He and his wife, Patricia, live in Staten Island with their daughter, Elizabeth.

INDEX